HELLO, GOD!

Prayers for Small Children

written by
Lois Walfrid Johnson
and illustrated by
Judy Swanson

AUGSBURG PUBLISHING HOUSE
Minneapolis, Minnesota

TO
ANNA-LISA, ALYCIA, AND CATHY
WITH LOVE

Dear Parent:

Within the circle of your arms you hold God's gift to you, your child. You hold also your child's most formative moments and most impressionable years.

Yours is a memory-building time—a time to fulfill your responsibility to pass along another of God's gifts, the opportunity to pray. In doing so, you will help your child deal with the present and provide a tool with which to meet the future.

Yours is also a time for joy. Along with the gift of prayer, God offers the balance of laughter—laughter which can enable you to enjoy your child and the wonder of childhood.

In these conversations about everyday experiences you will find the child's sense of joy and wonder. Sometimes you may want to substitute your own words. Your child may find new things to pray about which aren't mentioned in these pages. Use these prayers to encourage free and spontaneous talks with God.

As you seek to place your child's hand within the hand of God, you and your child will grow in a deeper understanding of his love. Your child will learn from you that prayer is a part of life and that it is natural to say, "Hello, God."

HELLO, GOD

Copyright © 1975 Augsburg Publishing House

Library of Congress Catalog Card No. 75-4157

International Standard Book No. 0-8066-1482-X

Manufactured in the United States of America

My fingers like to say hello
to each other
whenever I fold my hands,
and I like to say hello
to you, God.
I'm glad I can talk with you
whenever I want.
Thank you for listening.

Thanks for giving me
to mommy and daddy,
and thanks for giving
mommy and daddy to me.
I'm glad you made us a family.

It's fun to visit
grandma and grandpa
or have them come
to stay with us.
They make me feel good
inside.
Thanks for the way
they love me, God.

I like the new baby
you sent to our house.
He has soft skin
and wants lots of milk.
Help me to take care of mommy
when she's tired
and needs someone big
like me.

Thank you for loving
all the little children
in the world
the way you love me.
Show me how to be a good friend
to others
now
and when I am grown up.

God,
you gave me ears
to hear the robins sing.
You gave me eyes
to see rainbows in the sky.
You gave me fingers
to feel my kitten's fur.
I like the way you made me.

It's great to stand on my head
and see things topsy-turvy.
You made things
so they look good
either upside down
or rightside up.

Yummy!
This food smells great!
Thanks for giving it to me,
and thanks for sending
the rain and sunshine
that made it grow.

I like to help mommy.
Today I cleaned the cupboards
for her.
Thanks for big cans
and little cans,
for jello and cereal boxes,
and for kettles that clatter
and bang.

I like farms, God.
Thanks for red barns
and yellow hay
and big green tractors.
Thanks for making
cows that moo-o-o-o,
lambs that baa-a-a-a,
and chickens that cluck,
cluck,
cluck.

It's fun to have tea parties
and balloons
and dress-up clothes.
It's fun to have dolls
to hold and rock.
Thanks, God,
for giving me good times.

Dear God,
bless the people
who wipe away my tears
when I cry.
They hug me
and make me feel happy
again.

Thank you, Jesus,
for being my friend.
I'm glad
that even when my other friends
can't come out to play
you're always with me.

Daddy has to go on a trip, God. Please be with him while he's gone, and bring him safely home again.

When I'm in a crowd
I feel very small.
Then daddy puts me
on his shoulders
and I can see
the wh-o-o-o-le world.
Thanks for daddy's strong arms.

Be with the people
who are sick and sad and hungry.
Show me how to share with them.
Help me so I don't waste anything
you have given me.

My friend broke my new toy
and I'm angry, God.
Help me to forgive him.
Make me feel better
so I want to play with him again.

Dear Lord,
I wish that I weren't sick.
I want to go outside and play,
but mommy says
my head is hot.
I'm glad you watch over me.
Please help me feel well soon.

Sometimes my hands are naughty
and I need to say I'm sorry.
Please forgive me, God,
and help my hands
to be good.

I'm big, Lord!
I got dressed all by myself
this morning.
I'm glad I could help mommy
so much.

I like going to Sunday school
to learn more about you, God.
I like visiting
your special house.
I'm glad you're with me
in my house
all week long.

You made a great world, Lord—
piles of leaves to jump in,
snow for building snowmen,
tulips that pop from the earth,
and the sun to watch me play.
Thank you!

Sometimes the thunder
sounds like people
clapping their hands.
Thank you, God,
that you're strong enough
to make the lightning flash
and the wind blow,
and that you're strong enough
to take care of me.

It's fun to hear cars beep
and buses and trucks honk,
but I need someone bigger
than I am
to help me cross busy streets.
Remind me to always
be careful.

Thanks for swings
and jungle gyms
and merry-go-rounds
and games like tag
or hide-and-seek.
I'm glad you gave me strong legs
so I can climb
and run in the wind.

God,
I like watching caterpillars,
puppies and ants.
I like feeling sunfish
tug at my line.
I like wiggling my toes
in the warm, soft sand.
Be with me
whenever I play.

You did a good thing
when you made water, God.
It's fun to splash
in the tub
and sail my boat
and little duck.

Father in heaven,
Be with all the people
who take care of me—
my mommy and daddy,
my brothers and sisters,
my grandma and grandpa,
my aunts and uncles and cousins,
and my babysitters.
I'm glad they love me.

God,
Bless the good things
I did today—
the picture I colored,
the dandelions I picked,
the table I set for mommy.
Thanks for being with me.

Thank you
for my soft animals
and warm blankets.
Thank you
for hands that tuck me
into bed at night.
Thank you for watching over me
while I sleep.
Goodnight, God.